LIGHTNING BOLT BOOKS™

The Supersmart Dolphin

Mari Schuh

Lerner Publications • Minneapolis

To Fairmont Elementary School

Lerner Publications Company
A division of Lerner Publishing Group, Inc.
241 First Avenue North
Minneapolis, MN 55401 USA

For reading levels and more information, look up this title at www.lernerbooks.com.

Library of Congress Cataloging-in-Publication Data

Names: Schuh, Mari C., 1975- author.
Title: The supersmart dolphin / Mari Schuh.
Description: Minneapolis : Lerner Publications, [2018] | Series: Lightning bolt books. Supersmart animals | Audience: Ages 6-9. | Audience: K t grade 3. | Includes bibliographical references and index.
Identifiers: LCCN 2017054021 (print) | LCCN 2017040241 (ebook) | ISBN 9781541525306 (eb pdf) | ISBN 9781541519817 (lb : alk. paper) | ISBN 9781541527614 (pb : alk. paper)
Subjects: LCSH: Dolphins—Behavior—Juvenile literature. | Dolphins—Psychology—Juvenile literature.
Classification: LCC QL737.C432 (print) | LCC QL737.C432 S388 2018 (ebook) | DDC 599.53—dc23

LC record available at https://lccn.loc.gov/2017054021

Manufactured in the United States of America
1-44317-34563-11/17/2017

Table of Contents

Meet the Dolphin

Two dolphins leap out of the water. They sail through the air. Then they dive deep into the ocean.

Dolphins live in oceans and rivers around the world. Dolphins are social animals. They often live in groups, swimming and hunting together.

Smart Dolphins

Dolphins talk to one another using clicks, whistles, and squeals. Each dolphin makes its own whistle. Dolphins know one another from these whistles.

Echoes tell dolphins where to find squid, a common food for dolphins.

Dolphins also make clicking sounds that help them find things. The sounds bounce off objects and become echoes. Dolphins listen for the echoes. They tell dolphins where a thing is.

Dolphins are smart in many ways. They have long memories. They can remember other dolphins after being apart twenty years.

These pink dolphins might remember one another even after years apart!

Some bottlenose dolphins use sea sponges as tools! They put the sponges on their beaks as they hunt. The sponges protect their beaks from rocks and coral.

This dolphin swims with a sea sponge in its mouth.

Dolphins work together
when they hunt. They
sometimes form a circle
around a group of fish. The
dolphins trap the fish so
they can easily eat them.

Dolphins have saved people's lives. Dolphins have kept swimmers away from sharks.

Many people enjoy seeing dolphins up close.

The Life of a Dolphin

Dolphins live their whole lives in water. Their long, smooth bodies help them swim quickly. Most dolphins are less than 10 feet (3 m) long.

Large dolphins called orcas can be 26 feet (8 m) long!

Female dolphins give birth to one calf at a time. A calf drinks its mother's milk for two years or more.

This dolphin baby trails its mother in the water.

Calves stay with their mother for three or more years. Another adult dolphin may also stay near the pair. This dolphin helps the mother care for her baby.

Two dolphins may work together to raise a calf.

Orcas are known for being fierce hunters.

Dolphins live long lives in oceans and rivers. Many bottlenose dolphins live about twenty years. Orcas may live to be eighty years old.

Dolphins in Danger

Some kinds of dolphins are in danger of going extinct. Too much fishing in some areas leaves fewer fish for dolphins to eat. And dolphins can get caught in fishing nets.

Dolphins can die from pollution in rivers and oceans. Dams in rivers separate dolphins from the food they need.

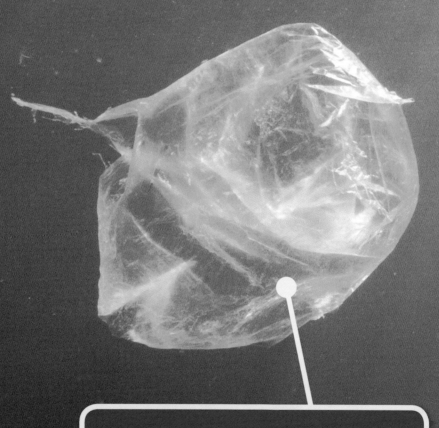

Plastic can harm ocean life.

People are working hard to keep dolphins safe. Some people help dolphins that are stranded on beaches. Others work to make new fishing rules so dolphins aren't trapped in nets.

Reusable bags can help keep plastic out of oceans.

People are working to make the oceans cleaner. They also study dolphins to learn how to help these animals even more.

This young person is picking up trash on a beach to keep the ocean clean for dolphins.

Dolphin Diagram

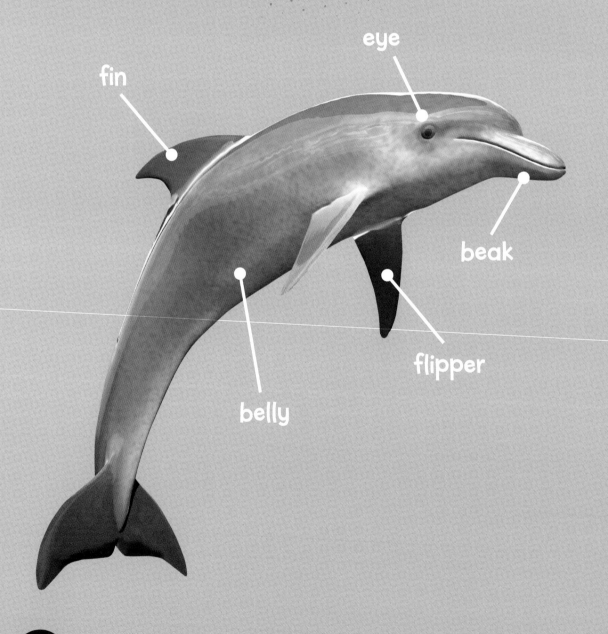

eye

fin

beak

belly

flipper

Fun Facts

- Bottlenose dolphins have undone knots in fishing nets.

- Dolphins can recognize themselves in mirrors. Only people and a few other animals have this skill!

- Dolphins have been trained to find and pick up lost equipment in the ocean.

Glossary

beak: a mouth structure that sticks out from the rest of the body

calf: a young dolphin

coral: a stony object made up of the skeletons of certain sea animals

extinct: having died out

pollution: materials that harm Earth's water, air, and land

sea sponge: a springy material that forms the skeleton of some ocean animals. Pieces of this material can be found in the ocean.

social: living in groups

Further Reading

Dolphin Research Center: Dolphin Facts for Kids
https://dolphins.org/kids_dolphin_facts

Dolphins World: Dolphin Facts for Kids
http://www.dolphins-world.com/dolphin-facts-for
-kids/

Franco, Betsy. *A Spectacular Selection of Sea Critters: Concrete Poems*. Minneapolis: Millbrook Press, 2015.

National Geographic Kids: Bottlenose Dolphin
http://kids.nationalgeographic.com/animals
/bottlenose-w/#world-oceans-day-dolphins
.jpg

Silverman, Buffy. *Can You Tell a Dolphin from a Porpoise*? Minneapolis: Lerner Publications, 2012.

Swanson, Jennifer. *Absolute Expert: Dolphins*. Washington, DC: National Geographic Kids, 2018.

Index

Photo Acknowledgments

The images in this book are used with the permission of: Potapov Alexander/Shutterstock.com, p. 2; muratart/Shutterstock.com, p. 4; Lance Sagar/Shutterstock.com, p. 5; Andrea Izzotti/Shutterstock.com, p. 6; Aleksandrs Marinicevs/Shutterstock.com, p. 7; Anirut Krisanakul/Shutterstock.com, p. 8; Yann hubert/Shutterstock.com, p. 9; wildestanimal/Shutterstock.com, p. 10; Ramon Harkema/Shutterstock.com, p. 11; Christian Musat/Shutterstock.com, p. 12; vkilikov/Shutterstock.com, p. 13; Paulphin Photography/Shutterstock.com, p. 14; Jen Helton/Shutterstock.com, p. 15; Petr Svarc/imageBROKER/Getty Images, p. 16; Tracey Jones Photography/Shutterstock.com, p. 17; Ariel Skelley/DigitalVision/Getty Images, p. 18; Chaleow Ngamdee/Shutterstock.com, p. 19; ArchMan/Shutterstock.com, p. 20; Tory Kallman/Shutterstock.com, p. 23.

Front cover: J & C Sohns/Picture Press/Getty Images.

Main body text set in Billy Infant regular 28/36. Typeface provided by SparkType.

ARE WE THERE YET?

Can you follow this maze and help the Johnsons get to the MOTEL?
Watch out for fallen trees, potholes, and garbage barges!

SILLY SANDWICH

At the Royal Diner, they serve a sandwich filled with everything!
Can you find 10 items in this sandwich that are *not* food?

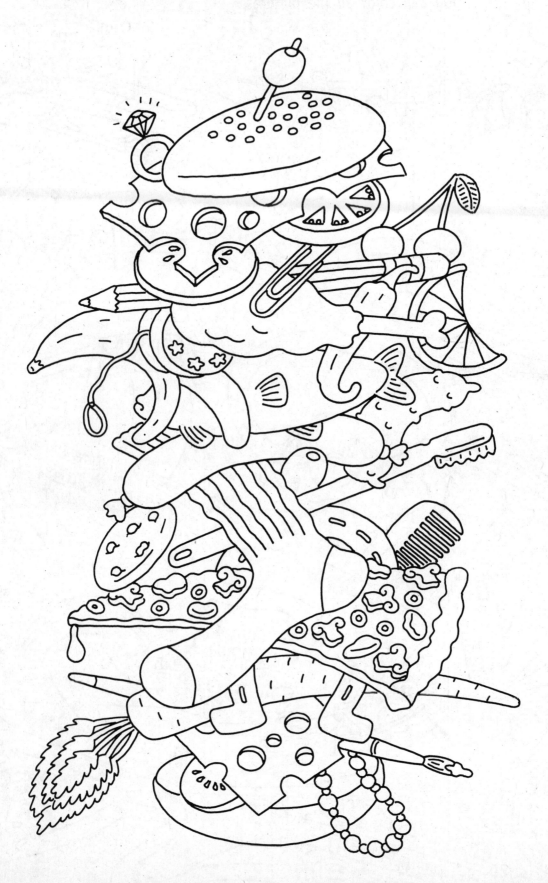

FLY ME

Circle only the objects and creatures that can fly.
You can color *all* the pictures.

TRICKY TRAVEL BINGO

As you travel in your car, look for the objects pictured below. As soon as you see the object, put an X through the picture square. We've done one of them for you.

COW	MOTORCYCLE	BRIDGE	CHINESE RESTAURANT	SCHOOL BUS
TRACTOR	MOVIE THEATER	BOWLING ALLEY	SAME CAR AS YOURS	WEATHER VANE
PIZZA SHOP	LAWN ANIMALS	U F O	GAS STATION	CLOTHESLINE
GARBAGE CAN	FARM	MAILBOX	DOG	BOAT
TRAILER	ICE-CREAM PARLOR	WELL	BICYCLE	MOTEL

CRAZY MIXED-UP TRAVEL PHOTOS

These travel photos are all mixed up. Can you put each person back together again by matching the right pieces in each column?

SNAPPY SOUVENIRS

Susie collected lots of souvenirs during her trip across America. Draw a line to connect each souvenir to the state where Susie bought it.

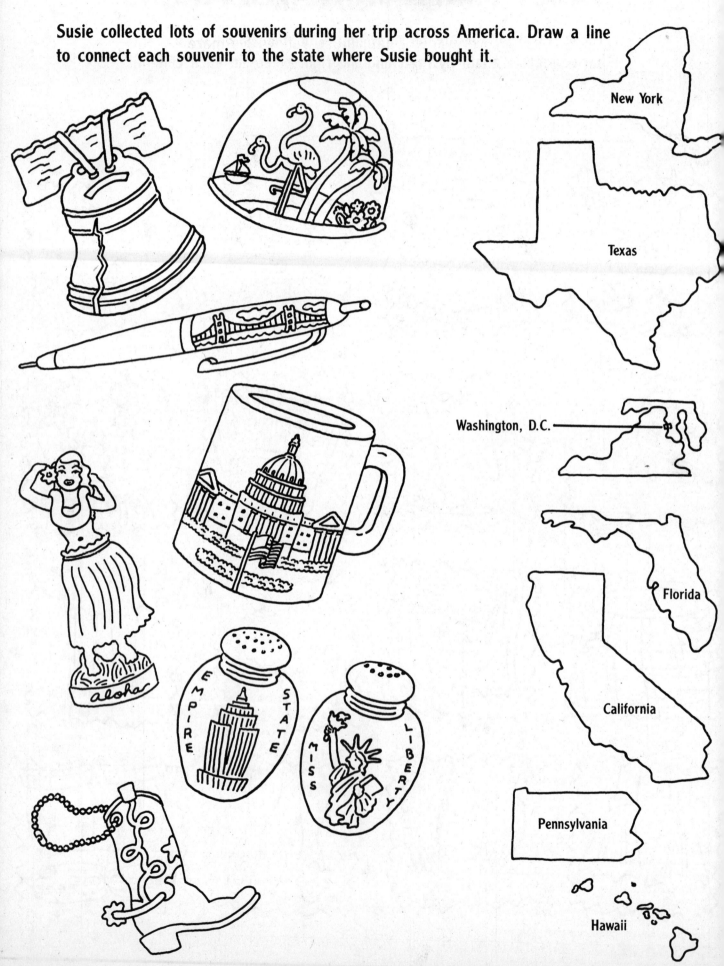

FOOD FINDER

Hungry Hal wants a hamburger. Follow this maze
to help Hal find Burger World.

INSTANT PICTURE

What is Johnny's favorite way to travel? To find out, color every
section that has two dots with your favorite color crayon.

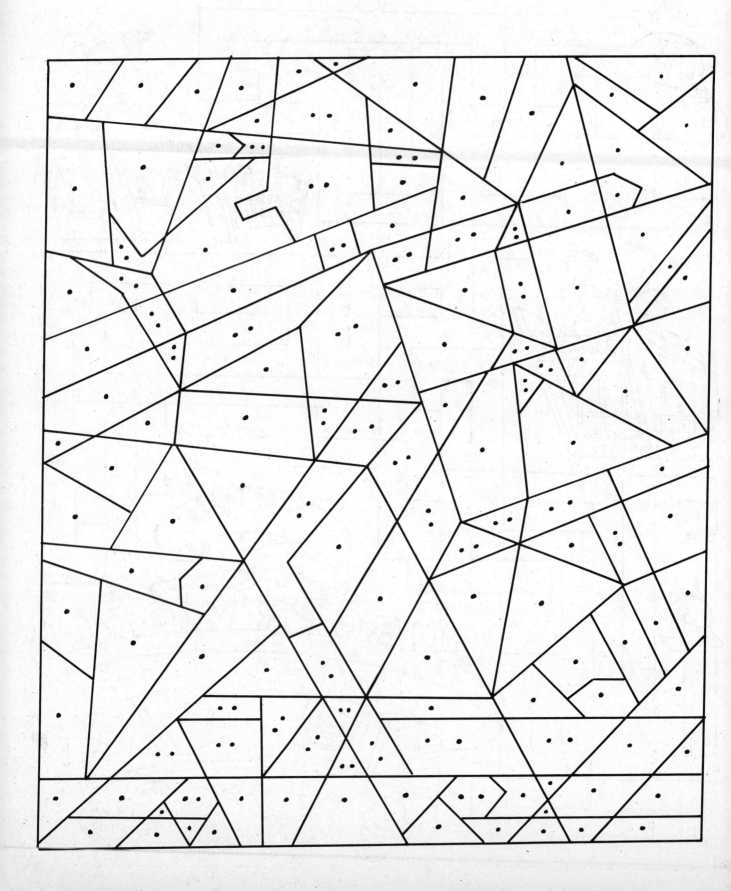

FREQUENT FLIERS

Who is flying the dinosaur balloon?
Follow the tangled lines to find out.

WHERE'S GUS?

It's a busy day at Gus's Gaseteria, and no one can find Gus!

Can you find him? (You'll know him by his hat.) You can also look for:
a bicycle pump, a water can, a fish, a bucket, a unicycle, a cat,
a faucet, a clock, a pillow, a wrench, and a sock.

DEF PET

Connect the dots to find out what Jerry brought back from his vacation.

BACKSEAT BOGGLE

Come join Jenny, Jon, and Barky in the backseat of their car.
Look at the picture carefully. Then turn the page and see
how much you can remember.

EXAMPLE: Circle the dog that matches the one in the picture.

Circle the picture in each row that matches the picture on page 17.

ART-O-MATIC

What animal is this? Color the picture using the following code to find the answer.

1 = pink 2 = green 3 = yellow 4 = brown 5 = blue 6 = gray 7 = black

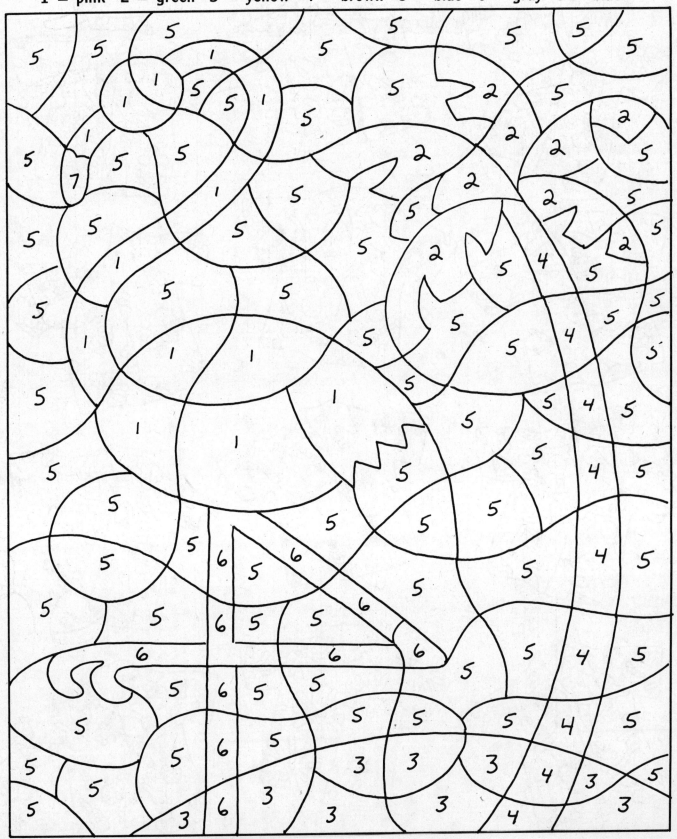

MIX AND MATCH

Can you find the two shirts that look exactly alike?

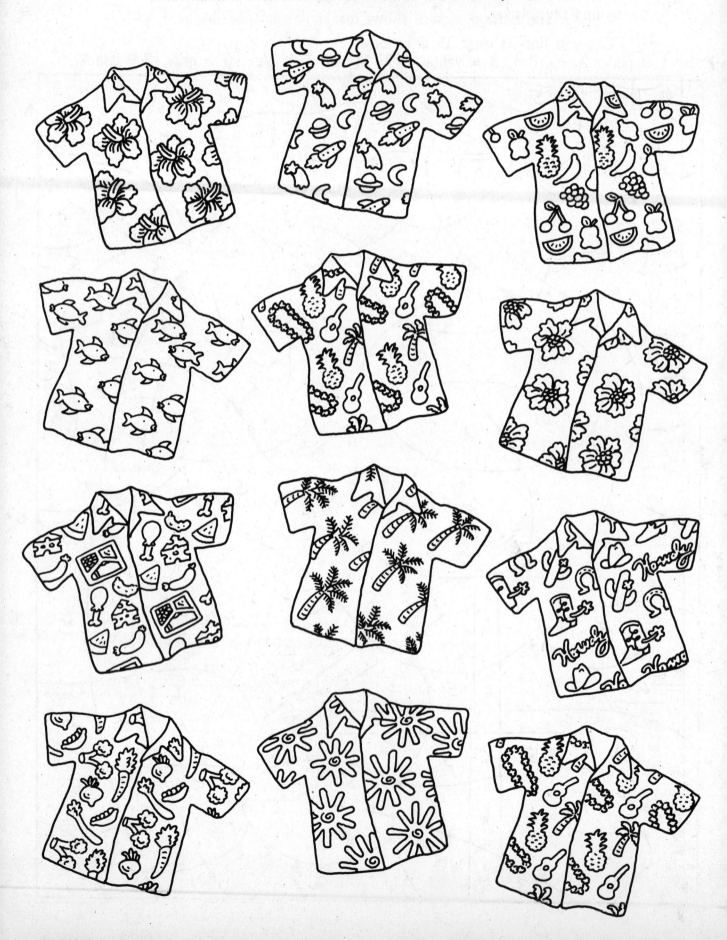

BEAR SCARE

The top picture shows the Smiths' campsite before a bear came visiting. The bottom picture shows the campsite after the bear left. Can you find at least 15 differences between the two pictures?

COOLER FOOLER

The Franklins are packing some food for a long car trip. Circle the items they can put in their cooler.

HONK IF YOU LOVE SLURPEES

Lovely SHAMPOO

BIG BELCH Cola

Mr. Tooth TOOTHPASTE
DELAY DECAY TODAY

Juicy PICKLES

FLAKE-O'S CEREAL

DOGGY TREATS

Bug Off!
BUG SPRAY

IT'S YUMMY!
CAKE
CAKE

A-MAZE-ING MINI-GOLF

Can you help Mimi complete this miniature golf course?

START

FINISH

DINER DILEMMA

Things at the Royal Diner are a little mixed up.
How many wrong things can you find in this scene?

MIXED-UP TRAVEL TALE

These pictures of the Fleegle family vacation are out of order. Can you put the pictures in the right order? Place the numbers 1, 2, 3, 4, 5, or 6 in the circle at the bottom of each picture.

BILL'S BOARD

Bill has been painting this billboard all morning. Use your imagination and help him draw the rest of the picture.

S IS FOR SEASHORE

Stuart is swallowing shrimp at the Seafood Shack.

Can you find other things that begin with the letter S in this seashore scene?

TRAFFIC JAM

It's rush hour on the Beantown Bridge. Match the empty vehicle with the person who rides in it.

ANSWERS

page 3

page 4

page 5

page 6

page 7

page 9

page 10
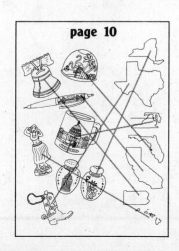

page 11

page 12

page 13

pages 14-15

page 16

page 18

page 19

page 20

page 21

page 22

page 23

page 26

page 30

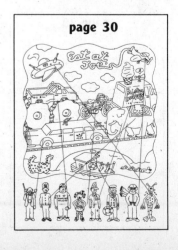